DON'T WASTE MY TIME

How To Beat All Your Competition on YouTube

BOBBY CROSBY
Illustrations by Remy "Eisu" Mokhtar

DON'T WASTE MY TIME
How To Beat All Your Competition On YouTube
by Bobby Crosby

Published by
Keenspot Entertainment
Los Angeles, CA
E-Mail: keenspot@keenspot.com
Web: www.keenspot.com

For Keenspot
CEO & EiC Chris Crosby
PRESIDENT Bobby Crosby

ISBN 978-1-954-36600-8
First Printing, September 2021
PRINTED IN CANADA

For everyone who hasn't yet
asked me how to do YouTube.

TABLE OF CONTENTS

INTRODUCTION

Introductions are bad. Don't do them.

CHAPTER ONE

THE FAILURE TO TRY

The goal of this book is not only for you to make a living from YouTube, but for it to be so comfortable that you never have to work again.

A lot of people see YouTube as a lottery, a quick chance to post some funny video that goes viral and makes you a star. And that happens. But the real winners are the ones who don't need viral videos, who don't need clickbait, who don't need luck. They beat their competition by consistently uploading entertaining content that a dedicated audience wants to see.

The good news is that you're already better than at least 10% of your competition. How do I know that? 1. You can read. 2. You care enough about doing well that you've started to read this book.

Far too many YouTubers barely try at all. They post random videos that don't even entertain themselves. This includes many very successful YouTubers, who have either given up at this stage of their career, or who are so naturally talented that effort was never required for them to build an audience.

There's nothing a viewer hates more than when a video makes it clear that it's not even trying to entertain them, and most YouTube videos are full of moments like that — random silences that go on too long or shaky camera work in a shot that didn't need to be in the video. Moments like these are begging the audience to stop watching, and most of your competition includes several of them in every video they make.

In some of these cases, the YouTuber actually is trying hard and they have no clue that they're doing anything wrong. This is because they overestimate the attention span of their audience and they're not editing tightly enough. Almost all YouTubers should edit tighter, even some who have Diamond Play

Buttons (10 million subscribers). People's attention spans are getting shorter and they're always ready to switch to your opponent if you bore them for even one second.

Why do so many YouTubers fail to try? Because they think it's a lottery, which doesn't take any effort — you just have to buy a ticket, by posting a video. They think it's a get-rich-quick scheme, but it's not — it's a get-rich-quick job, which takes a lot of hard work to initially secure. If done correctly, after two or three years of a tough grind, you'll be able to live off your existing archive of videos for the rest of your life, like the creator of a popular TV show that goes into syndication.

I can tell you how to do this because I've done it.

In the past four years, I've only worked about five hours per week on YouTube and I've made several million dollars. In August of 2020, I uploaded zero videos, worked zero hours, and my channel made $43,097. In June of 2021, which is the most recently completed month as this book goes to print, I worked about 10 hours per week and my channel made $172,007. That's for one month, and from YouTube ad revenue alone. And all of this was done without anything going viral, without any bad clickbait, without any collaborations from bigger YouTubers, without heavily promoting merchandise, without doing many sponsored videos, without photoshopping any thumbnails, and without ever buying any advertising. It was also accomplished with types of videos that aren't normally popular. Almost all of my videos are either real life softball games with friends, or gaming videos where I play a baseball video game very poorly.

The short answer for why my videos are popular is "humorous commentary with tight editing." The long answer is this book. And the advice in this book will work for any kind of channel.

If you're thinking that there must be a catch, you're right. There's three.

1. You must be at least a moderately entertaining person.

    If no one's ever told you that you're funny, you're probably not going to make a living on YouTube. On a scale of 1-10 as an entertainer, you need to be at least a 5.

2. You need to actually follow the advice in this book, and not just some of it.

    When diets fail, it's practically never because the diet plan was bad — it's because you didn't follow the plan, because you weren't motivated enough to stay on it, or you changed an important aspect and thought it wouldn't make a difference.

Think of this book as the recipe for a fancy dish that you've never cooked before. Let's say you're making beef bourguignon, and you do everything perfectly, except you replace the 3 ½ tablespoons of butter with 3 ½ tablespoons of poison instead. Of course you'd never do that, but you might not realize what could be poisonous to your YouTube channel. Better to be safe than sorry.

3. The goal, as stated, is for you to get rich from YouTube, and unfortunately the only way to do that is to devote a huge amount of time early on.

Ideally you'd be treating this like a full time job from the start, but you probably already have one of those — or school, or both. It varies based on what kind of videos you do, but to properly make this advice work, it would initially require a minimum of 15 hours per week. And, as soon as possible, after achieving some success and getting comfortable, you would need to increase your workload dramatically. Before this can become a 5-hour per week job, it needs to be a 50-hour per week job for a significant length of time at some point, like it was for me in 2016.

If you can do all three of those things, it's impossible for you to fail, unless your videos are literally about watching paint dry. There's an audience for almost everything.

Most big YouTubers wish they started their channel earlier, so they could have even more years in their dream job and more money in the bank. But that doesn't mean you should rush to post videos as soon as possible. The title of this chapter — *The Failure to Try* — does not refer to people who have never tried YouTube. It refers to people who have tried, but not hard enough, or in the wrong way. It's imperative that you do it right, not that you do it fast.

If you're brand new to YouTube, or if you don't currently upload regularly, you should take at least a month to study this book and prepare before making a video. It's far worse to put up a bad video than to put up no video at all. In many ways you should act like you're producing a TV show, and no network or streaming service would release a series if they were completely unsure of its quality. You have to make test videos and have test screenings — even if you're the only one watching.

If you're already posting regularly and have a decent sized audience, you should wait until you've finished the book and have fully absorbed all the necessary changes before implementing any of them. Then do them all at once. Otherwise, the recipe will be wrong and you might come to false conclusions about the effectiveness of the advice.

It's absolutely crucial to have the right mindset going into this about the type of effort required. That's why this is the first chapter. It's not a mislabeled introduction. It's the key ingredient that allows all the others to work.

And by the way, this book assumes that you're already pretty knowledgeable about YouTube. I won't waste your time covering things that you can easily google and that you probably already have. In my experience, books like this are usually 50% autobiography, 25% biographies of other successful people, and 25% stuff you already know. This isn't one of those. I've been in your spot and I'm not going to subject you to another experience like that.

Most of you have already tried YouTube, and you picked up this book in the hopes that it would give you a few magical secrets that would double or triple your subscriber count. The rest of you are a bit more hopeful, not having yet faced the harsh reality of how impossible it can seem to break through on YouTube. But even for most of the newcomers, your dreams only reach the height of quitting your job and doing YouTube full time. You need to set your sights higher, which will help you realize how hard you have to work to get there.

Your goal shouldn't be to triple your subscriber count. It should be to multiply it by 1,000. Your goal shouldn't be to do YouTube full time. It should be to get so rich from YouTube that you can do anything you want in life, like maybe pursue a childhood dream. Being a YouTuber actually is the childhood dream for a huge amount of kids nowadays, and if you're one of them, I'm happy to help you achieve it. If you're older like me and had a different dream growing up, it's never too late to start.

I was 35 and broke when I started doing most of the things that I advise in this book, and in six months I went from getting 900,000 views in a month to 31 million. I had already been doing YouTube off and on for eight years and had found some success, but nowhere near enough to make a living from it. For January of 2016, YouTube paid me $1,230. For December of 2016, YouTube paid me $80,446. What made the difference? A million things, which I'll detail in this book, but the biggest change was that I finally started to actually try. I recognized what was possible and I challenged myself to achieve it.

I realize that it sounds so simple and obvious to say that you need to try — and don't worry, the advice gets a lot juicier after this — but the failure to try is the biggest problem that I see. YouTube has the power to completely change your life and you need to treat it with the respect that it deserves if you want it to change yours. It's not a lottery. It's not a scheme. It's Hollywood with an open door.

Throughout this book, you will learn skills to earn badges, and each badge represents a certain percentage of your competition that you're now better than simply for learning this one skill. Congratulations on achieving your first and most important badge.

You are now beating 20% of your competition.

CHAPTER TWO

THE BIG THREE

To be successful in most endeavors, you don't have to be great at what you do, and in some cases you don't even have to be good. You simply have to be better than your competition.

In 2005, I was looking to buy a used Xbox on eBay. After ten minutes of research, I made the obvious discovery that listings with photos sold for way more than those without. People don't trust what they can't see. Despite eBay's best efforts to get everyone to take pictures of their items, lots of people still didn't do it back then — because they didn't have a smartphone.

At first I was happy to save a little money by finding the most trustworthy listing that didn't have a photo. But then I kept noticing more mistakes that hurt the sale price, like bad titles and short descriptions. I also discovered that if the Xbox included a large number of games, it would sell for far more than it should, based on how much you could separately buy a lot of used games for.

So instead of buying one Xbox, I bought 30 of them over the next few months, along with about 1,000 games. Using what I learned from my research, I re-sold them on eBay for a total profit of around $3,000.

Almost every item on eBay has a picture nowadays, and they've taken various steps to essentially eliminate horrible listings, so it's impossible to do now what I did back then, which was to exploit the weaknesses of my competition.

But it's not impossible on YouTube.

YouTube in 2021 is like eBay in 2005.

Your competition is full to the brim with major weaknesses that you can take advantage of. And the nice thing for you is that it should stay this way for many years to come, because the biggest problems with YouTube videos aren't obvious, like the lack of photos were on eBay. The introduction of the iPhone mostly fixed eBay's picture problem, but I can't imagine there's anything like that coming for YouTube. Unless this book sells 10 million copies.

Most people in the know, including YouTube itself, will tell you that improving your Watch Time is the best thing you can do to be successful on YouTube. What they don't know, or what they're not willing to share, are the best ways to improve it.

Watch Time is the amount of time that a viewer spends watching a video. So if you have a 10 minute video that gets 1,000 views, and if the average viewer watches half of it, or 5 minutes, that video has 5,000 minutes of Watch Time.

YouTube has an all-important secret algorithm that determines which videos show up high in search results or get recommended to others. This algorithm will decide your fate, and the biggest thing YouTube has revealed about it is the importance of Watch Time.

There are two key stats related to Watch Time:

1. Total Watch Time — the total number of minutes (or hours or days or years) that your videos have been seen.

YouTube holds this stat in such high regard because it's the best indication that a viewer will watch more of your videos and stay on YouTube for longer, which is their ultimate goal.

2. Watch Time Percentage, also known as audience retention.

    Way more than likes or dislikes, this metric is the best indication YouTube has for how good any particular video is, because the higher percentage of a video that someone watches, the more they like it. This stat is more meaningful for longer videos. It's more impressive if someone sits through all of a 15 minute video than all of a 15 second video.

It's a combination of those two metrics that drive YouTube's recommendations. YouTube wants you to watch good videos, but they prefer if you watch good videos from channels that have lots of other good videos available for you to keep watching until you accidentally fall asleep and drop your phone on your face.

To improve Total Watch Time, these are the main things you can do: make more videos, make your videos more binge-worthy, make better videos, and make longer videos (but not at the expense of quality). And to improve your Watch Time Percentage, you simply have to make better videos.

So that's our main focus for the first half of this book — how to crush the Watch Time stats by making videos that people can't stop watching.

I've always loved stats. When I was a little kid, whenever I got sick, I made myself feel better by reading a big book of baseball records. More than anything else, that's what calmed me down and made me feel at peace. So when I finally noticed the treasure trove of analytics data that YouTube provides to all creators, I took that as an opportunity to crack the code, to do my own version of sabermetrics and discover the secret strategies that are most valuable on YouTube.

I found them.

Lots of them.

Some have been found by others, but most of them, including all three of what I call The Big Three, are rarely talked about anywhere.

I learned these secrets from a deep dive of my own analytics, combing through the data of over a thousand videos, and then I confirmed them through trial and error over the course of making another thousand videos. Along the way, various YouTuber friends allowed me to check their analytics, where I found the exact same things.

These are not theories. This is the result of years of research on thousands of videos from multiple popular channels.

Various discoveries were made across all categories, like the best time of day to post a video and the best types of titles and thumbnails. But the real pot of gold came from studying the audience retention graphs for each video, which show you the exact percentage of viewers who are still watching for each second of the video, so you can see when they leave. Sometimes the line graph actually shoots up, and that means people are re-watching those parts of the video or skipping ahead to those parts. Things can be learned from that, but the main knowledge comes from the sudden drops, and your goal is to eliminate those completely.

Whenever you see a sharp decline in the retention graph, it doesn't simply mean that people disliked that part of your video and stopped watching. It often means they hated that part so much that they'll never watch any of your videos again.

I painstakingly went through every video I had ever made and wrote down what happened to cause every sudden drop that I found. I also noted exactly how big the drop was. Initially it was hard to tell in some cases why the drops occurred, but patterns emerged over time and they all became clear.

Before we get into The Big Three, the three most important revelations from the retention graphs, let me give you a one paragraph overview of what I learned:

In every second of every video, you must, at the very least, make a clear attempt to entertain the audience. It doesn't even have to work. Simply by trying, you will succeed. The audience always rewards effort, because they so rarely see it.

But you might be surprised by what constitutes effort in the mind of the average YouTube viewer. There are many specific things you must do to show that you're trying, starting with this:

Nonstop Dialogue

This is already a very short book, but if I was forced to write a version that was only two words long, those words would be "Nonstop dialogue." The three-word version would be "Never stop talking." Whenever anyone asks me for YouTube advice, this is the first thing I tell them.

In one key way, YouTube is much more like radio than television, and it's this: dead air is the worst thing you can have. And just like the radio, unless we're hearing an entire song, that air time needs to be filled with spoken words.

Silence truly is the silent killer. It kills videos and entire channels without the YouTuber ever realizing it was there. In my retention graph studies, silence didn't cause the sharpest declines, but it was by far the most common reason for any drop, accounting for more than half of them.

At first it seemed a little weird to talk nonstop for every second of an entire video, but I stopped questioning it when I saw the dramatic change in my numbers. My Watch Time Percentage skyrocketed, along with my views and subscribers and everything else that's supposed to be high. No single change has ever boosted my channel as much as this.

If you're wondering about sequences without dialogue where music is playing, like a musical montage, those aren't quite as bad as both a lack of dialogue and a lack of music, but almost. Background music is often a good idea for you to talk over, but once you stop talking, it can't do much by itself to stop the viewers from leaving.

If you were to ask viewers why they like nonstop dialogue, they couldn't tell you, because they don't know they like it. It's a mostly subconscious thing. When someone stops watching a video during a long silence, if you asked them why, they'd say, "I don't know, got bored." I've thought about it for years, and I think there's three main reasons:

1. When you stop talking, it often seems like you're bored, and if the viewer thinks you've lost interest in what you're doing, then they've totally lost interest.

2. In a video where you're talking most of the time, the silences can seem like filler, like you only used those moments to increase the video's length, most commonly so you can reach enough minutes to include midroll ads.

3. A prolonged silence gives the audience permission to leave. As long as you keep talking, you're holding them captive. Unless it's an incredible video that they've been looking forward to, like the trailer for a huge film, YouTube viewers are ready to leave any video at a moment's notice. There's a small part of the viewer that actually wants your video to be bad, so they can move on to the million other things they want to watch. And if they're brand new to your videos, they're even more critical, because they already have a crowded rotation of channels that they love, so you'll have to be perfect for them to make space for you. Silence is their excuse to reject you. They'll usually give you

a chance as long as you keep talking to them. So never stop.

How long can you go without dialogue? One second. Anything beyond that is too long.

Other than music videos, are there any exceptions? Probably. But if I were you, I wouldn't risk making an exception until you're immensely popular. And it's impossible to tell you what the exceptions are — they show up randomly, organically. I used to often make a funny face of the biggest frown you'll ever see with bulging eyes, which I'd stare into the camera with for several seconds. After learning the importance of nonstop dialogue, I still made that face occasionally, because it was well liked, but I wouldn't hold the stare quite as long.

You might be asking why lots of hugely successful YouTubers don't follow this advice, why they're silent so often in their videos, and I have three things to say to that:

1. They're almost certainly extremely talented, and extreme talent can overcome almost anything.

2. It's the stars with experience who know how to recognize those rare moments when silence works.

3. Just imagine how much more successful they'd be if they did follow this advice. The common misconception that I hate more than any other is that super popular things must have never done anything wrong. Even some of the most popular things in history could have been way more popular with a few changes. How much more popular would *Game of Thrones* be if the final season wasn't horrible? Nothing is perfect. There's always room for improvement.

I understand if you're hesitant to follow some of my advice, if it isn't exactly what you had in mind for your channel, but think of it this way: The advice in this book lowers the degree of difficulty for you to succeed. In my opinion, to use a golf metaphor, it's the equivalent of making the entire green the hole, just for you, while everyone else has to actually putt. You might also have to wear ridiculous looking golf pants, but I think that's worth it to win the Masters.

You won't have any objection to doing the second of The Big Three, but it's tougher than it sounds:

Never Confuse the Audience

Almost nothing angers a viewer more than confusing them. If you say something they don't get, and then you fail to immediately clear it up, they're gone.

What's confusing? Anything the audience doesn't understand. The most common culprit is when the YouTuber refers to something that happened in one of their previous videos without fully explaining it. This doesn't inspire the viewer to go find that video. It inspires them to never watch you again.

To a large degree, you have to treat every video you make like it's the first time the audience has ever seen you, because it always is for some of them. And as you get more popular and start showing up often in recommended videos, a high percentage of your viewers will always be brand new people.

Have you ever tried a new channel for the first time and heard the YouTuber say something that made you go "Wait, what?" If so, do you remember what happened after that? I do — you stopped watching the video and totally forgot you had ever seen it.

Your enemy is "Wait, what?" You despise "Wait, what?" At all costs, you must prevent making your viewers say "Wait, what?"

There are a million ways to be confusing. You have to be on the lookout for them at all times.

If you're in the middle of a series, you should give a simple recap of what's happened so far early in each video. I've done over 800 episodes of a series where I play through the entire career of a baseball player modeled after myself. He's just like me, if I was good looking and good at baseball. Near the start of most episodes, I'll say something like this: "It's the 2034 season, Crosby's 20th year in the majors. He's won 18 World Series rings, he's hit over 3,000 home runs, and he's the greatest athlete in the history of sports." Some viewers might be put off by how ridiculous that sounds, but at least they're not confused.

Another common cause for confusion is dialogue that can't be understood, often occurring in vlogs where the speaker is too far away from the mic or where there's lots of background noise. You can't allow this to happen. If the hard to understand line is absolutely hilarious, throw a subtitle on the screen so we can at least read it, but in general you want to simply cut out such things. This often means entire videos can't be used. Never film under poor conditions for audio, and always tell your friends to talk loudly enough so they can be clearly understood.

I could write 500 pages of ways to confuse the audience, so you must be able to recognize them and prevent them on your own. You should always put yourself in the shoes of someone who's seeing your videos for the first time. Every video you make needs to be for them more than anyone else. That's the best way to avoid confusion and to build an audience.

The last of The Big Three is impossible to fully accomplish, but you have to try:

Never Annoy the Audience

I say "never" because I guess that should be the goal, but the only way to conceivably achieve it is to be incredibly boring, and you don't want to do that. No matter what you do, some people will find it annoying, especially if you're trying to entertain them. I rarely have any drops in my retention graphs anymore, but when I do, most of them fall under this category. It's usually an attempt at humor that fails. And there's nothing you can do about that — you can't stop trying to be funny. What you can do is limit your level of annoyance as much as possible.

There are thousands of ways that YouTubers are annoying, and here are some of the top offenders that you need to keep out of your videos:

Shaky camera work is unacceptable. I'll never understand why so many YouTubers think it's fine. Sure, once in a blue moon it'll be necessary to include a brief shaky shot, if we absolutely need to hear the dialogue from that moment, or if the shakiness itself makes the scene hilarious, but you can't regularly include these types of shots. They're not only annoying, but they literally make some people sick.

You need decent sounding audio. It doesn't have to be incredible, but it can't be annoying, especially when you're screaming into the mic. And yes, screaming by itself will of course annoy some people, but it's often worth it to make your videos more exciting and genuine. Some YouTube stars refer to themselves as professional screamers. But it will do more harm than good if you're blowing out their eardrums with scratchy sounding screams. You can fix this problem in the same way that you can fix any technical problem — google it like crazy and mess with the settings until you get it right. This is a big reason why you should take at least a month before posting your first video.

If you're using multiple layers, like gaming videos where we're seeing the gameplay footage and a face cam, everything needs to be synced up perfectly, especially your lips to the microphone track. For me personally, nothing's more annoying than the lip sync being off. I can't watch that for two seconds without turning it off.

On the subject of face cams for gaming videos, three more key points:

1.   Be very careful to place the face cam in the least annoying spot possible that still looks decent. For reference, look at where other YouTubers put their faces while playing the same video game. But don't blindly copy them, since they might be doing it wrong. Make sure not to block any important info, like the score of the game.

2.   This one is huge and it will give you a big advantage over your competition: Make your face cam as large as you reasonably can on the screen, and, more importantly, make sure that you're zoomed in close enough so that we're mostly just seeing your face itself in that face cam. A giant percentage of YouTubers, including lots of very popular ones, use tiny face cams that look like security camera footage of their room, which completely eliminates the very purpose of the face cam. The whole point is for the audience to see your reactions, to get to know you better, to feel closer to you. And most of them are watching on the tiny screen of their phone. They can't root for you if they can't see you. And always remember that it doesn't matter what the video looks like in your editing software — it only matters what it will end up looking like on a phone. This means you have to make everything bigger

than you might initially think, like your face cam and any text you put on the screen.

3. Make sure that your face is looking towards the gameplay action on the screen. For example, if your face cam is in the bottom left corner, your face should be looking up towards the top right corner, so it looks like you're watching the game. This might require putting your camera in different places based on what game or mode you're playing, which can be frustrating, but it's worth it to not annoy the audience by looking offscreen at their thumb holding the phone.

If you add in sound effects to your videos, make certain that none of them are too loud or annoying, especially if you're placing them in an unexpected spot. I generally recommend not using sound effects, unless you're positive you're doing it correctly.

Recurring features and catchphrases are great, but if it's not something that's clearly entertaining, you should try to avoid repetition with your dialogue. To use another baseball example, it's good to have a unique home run call that you bring back sometimes in key moments, but it's extremely annoying if you say "That ball is crushed!" every time you hit a homer. You've gotta mix it up.

Similar to the confusion dilemma, there are endless examples of how to be annoying, so you'll have to figure out how to recognize them. You should study your own retention graphs periodically to try to pinpoint things that your audience doesn't like, and you should also read all the comments on your videos, but be careful not to put too much stock in them. Viewers often ask for things that they don't realize they'd actually hate.

So that's The Big Three, and you'll notice that they're all about avoiding mistakes, because that's all you really have to do. It doesn't take incredible skill to become a YouTube star. You don't have to throw a football 70 yards or hit a baseball 500 feet. You just have to be vigilant about not doing anything stupid to piss off the viewers or make them feel like you've wasted their time. If you prove to them that you value their time, the rest will come easy.

Congratulations on earning three more badges!

You are now beating 55% of your competition.

CHAPTER THREE

THE ROTATION

More Americans watch YouTube than drink soda.

Over two billion people on Earth watch YouTube at least once a month.

As long as YouTube still exists, nothing is going to stop people from watching it. They're not just going to quit, even if all the videos on it were suddenly terrible. Most of them already are terrible. Which is why your chances to succeed are so high.

What you really need to do is get into the rotation of as many viewers as possible, and then stay in it as long as you can. Every viewer has a certain amount of channels that they follow regularly, that they'll eagerly check for new videos. That's their rotation. And within that rotation, they have favorites, including the channel they love the most, which I call their ace. It's good to be the ace, but it's not required. Anywhere in the rotation is fine. The whole trick is simply to get in it and stay in it, and here are some of the best ways to do that:

Never Post a Bad Video

When a viewer puts you in their rotation, it's like you're starting to date each other. It's more exciting early on, but it's also more precarious and easier to end at any moment. Whenever you get a lot of new subscribers in a short period of time, like from a collaboration or something going viral, those next few weeks are crucial for you to not give them any reason to dump you. The longer a relationship lasts, the worse of a crime you have to commit for them to break up with you. If your wife hears you tell an insensitive joke that she finds offensive, she might roll her eyes and shake her head, but if you told her that same exact joke on your first date, she might have never spoken to you again. It's imperative to avoid mistakes early on, and the biggest mistake a YouTuber can make is posting a genuinely bad video.

The most glaring example of a bad video is one that doesn't have any actual content in it, like an introductory video for your channel, or a brief update on why you haven't been posting lately. Every single video you upload must entertain the audience in some specific way. Unless your whole channel is like this and you're an incredible speaker or comedian, never post a video that's entirely just a "talking head," where you're talking to the camera the whole time without anything else of interest going on.

So, for your first video, instead of merely doing an introduction, you need to incorporate that introductory dialogue into the opening of a video that has actual content in it. And instead of posting a one minute update on your life, make a regular video like you'd normally do and give your update in that.

Other common examples of bad videos are ones where you significantly break any of The Big Three rules. If you're considering uploading a video that has lengthy silent sections without any dialogue, you should ask yourself if you feel like being dumped that day. Or if you feel like not being remotely appealing to anyone who's looking for a new relationship.

This is the main reason why you should be very careful with doing collaborations, because unexpected things can happen with new people that result in a bad video. This might cost you some opportunities, but I suggest making it very clear to all potential collaborators that you are under no obligation to actually post the video being made.

But if you ever do find yourself in the horrible situation of feeling completely compelled to post a bad video, you should do the opposite of clickbait and sabotage your own video to get as few views as possible. Use the most boring title and thumbnail you can think of and post it at midnight on a weekday. You should also make such a video as short as possible. It's less difficult to endure a bad experience if it's brief, like ripping off a band-aid.

People are often very confused by this advice, so let me be crystal clear: You do not want a lot of views for a bad video. Those views are doing you more harm than good, for two reasons:

1. If an existing subscriber sees it, there's a strong chance they'll dump you because of it, and this is also true even if the video in question was made years earlier and they just happen to be watching it now for the first time. Not many people notice when videos were uploaded — they just see it in their recommendations and play it — so you won't be cut any slack because it's old.

2. Much more importantly, if it's the first time someone has ever seen a video of yours, they won't put you in their rotation if the video is bad. And not only will they not put you in their rotation now, but they'll usually

never give you another chance. If they happen to see you recommended again, they won't try it because they'll remember how you wasted their time previously. On YouTube, even more so than everywhere else, you absolutely must make a good first impression.

Just imagine if there was an episode of *Friends* that was nothing like the others and featured Chandler talking to the camera for the entire half hour about cheese. Now imagine if that's the first episode you ever saw of *Friends*. Would you have ever watched another? At some point, the producers would realize their mistake and try to erase that episode from existence, like the 1978 *Star Wars Holiday Special*. It certainly wouldn't have made it to a streaming service.

It's sometimes not wise to do this when the video is part of a series, but if they're not in a series and if you're under no obligation to keep them up, you should remove (or make private) every bad video you've ever made. Even if a bad video is your most viewed video by far, that's actually more reason to delete it than to keep it up, because it means it's doing even more damage as it's seen by more and more people.

And if all of your videos are bad, remove them all and start your channel all over again.

Some of you might laugh at that and think it's crazy. It's not. After eight years of doing YouTube, I had 49 million views from 1,344 videos. I then removed all of them, for a variety of reasons, but mostly because my research made me realize they were bad. And removing all of my old videos is a big reason why I've had over 700 million views in the five years since then.

So this is a giant issue. It's not something to ignore and put your head in the sand about. You'll have to make some judgement calls on what counts as a bad video, and I suggest being very tough with your assessments.

Promote Binge-Watching

Viewers are far more likely to put you in their rotation if they're following a series of videos that you're posting. So, whenever you can make something a series, you should make it a series. I have over 2,400 videos on my channel and only three of them are not part of a series.

Not only should you try to make everything a series, but you should shout that fact from the rooftops. Put the number of each episode in the title and even more importantly in the thumbnail. Many large YouTubers disagree with this advice because they think new viewers won't want to start watching a series unless it's the first episode, so they'll ignore anything other than #1. They're mostly correct about that, but you need to do it anyway, because the benefits dramatically outweigh the costs.

If a new viewer (someone who's never watched you before) sees a big #37 in the thumbnail for one of your videos that's being recommended to them, here's what goes through their head:

"Wow, #37? Must be a good series if YouTube is recommending the 37th episode. Surprised I haven't heard of this YouTuber before. Damn, this might be good. But I don't want to start here — let's go find the first episode."

The interesting thing is that they might never actually get around to watching #37, but a decent percentage of them will watch the first five or more episodes of the series and then start watching the new ones as you continue to put them out. They might end up watching a thousand of your videos over the years all because of seeing a number in the thumbnail for a video they didn't even watch.

Let that sink in. This one's powerful. It's also one of the tips that you're most likely to ignore, so make sure you don't do that, because this advice is a key factor towards unlocking the passive income that everyone dreams of.

For successful YouTubers who don't follow this advice, who don't properly promote binge-watching, a huge percentage of them can only continue to thrive on YouTube if they're constantly putting out new videos, because no one's watching their old ones. I could list 50 YouTubers who have more subscribers than me and who have posted more videos than I have but who don't even get 10% as many views from their archives as I do. Essentially all of the views for their channels are coming from new videos. Mine's the opposite, where new videos are just a nice bonus. In the past five years, I've uploaded over 1,000 new videos, but I haven't even come close to having a single day where the majority of my channel's views came from new videos I put out that day.

If you want to make money while you're sleeping or on vacation, it's incredibly difficult to do so by making a bunch of short films that have no relation to each other. You must make shows that have lots of episodes. And if you actually are making shows that have lots of episodes, the last thing you want to do is make it seem like you're posting random short films instead.

You need each viewer to watch as many of your videos as possible, which they're far more likely to do if they know they're watching a series. If you can get 10 people to each watch 10 of your videos, that's better than getting 99 people to each watch one of your videos.

When a viewer sees an episode number, they mentally prepare themselves for the possibility of watching a bunch of videos. When they see a title and thumbnail that looks like a one-off, standalone video, they'll only prepare themselves to watch that. It's the difference between watching a series on Netflix or watching a feature film. And the more videos you watch from the same channel, the more likely you are to put them in your rotation.

And again, there are lots of huge YouTubers who don't do this for various reasons, and I'm not saying that they're all wrong for making that choice. There are exceptions to almost everything in life, and different people have different circumstances. The gigantic YouTubers rightfully care less about finding new viewers than they do about pleasing their current fan base, because they're so popular that there aren't many new viewers left for them to find. They're in the exact opposite situation as you, which requires a different approach.

The advice in this book is heavily about how to get your first million subscribers and how to get over 100 million views per year. Once you reach those levels, you can basically do anything you want.

The very nature of having a series means that the first episode will usually get the most views, including a high percentage from brand new viewers, so it's extremely important that every #1 video is good. About a dozen times I've completely re-shot the first episode of a series (only for my gaming videos) because it just wasn't entertaining enough, but I've almost never done that for any episode other than the first. The best way to get someone to binge-watch an entire series is to make the first episode incredible.

Make Test Videos

After finishing this book, no matter what stage you're at with YouTube or how good you are at following advice, you should make at least one test video that you have no plans to post, just so you can watch it carefully and make sure that you're not directly going against anything this book advises. You should also get a couple smart friends to read this book and watch your test video. If a mistake is found, make more test videos until you're certain you're doing everything right.

I've communicated some version of this book to dozens of people over the years, and this is what happens more than half the time: They thank me for the advice and act as if they're really excited about it, then they link me to their first new video, which doesn't come remotely close to following all of my advice and which usually breaks all three of the Big Three rules in the first minute.

Like I said at the start, this book will only work if you make sure that you're following all of the advice. Unless you're a 10 on the entertainer scale, in which case practically any approach will work. And here's how you know if you're a 10: If you're constantly being offered large sums of money to host awards shows, then you're probably a 10. If you've never received such an offer, you're not a 10.

Never Be Late

We'll talk at length in the next chapter about how you need a schedule for your videos, but whatever that schedule ends up being, you have to stick to it.

To use *Friends* again, just imagine if a new episode was supposed to air on Thursday at 8 PM, and instead NBC aired nothing at all, just a black screen. Depending on how big of a fan you are, most people could forgive one big error like that, but what if they did it again two weeks later? Even the biggest fans would start dropping out at that point, because it's just a slap in the face from the makers of the show that says they don't care about you or the work they're doing.

If you're thinking it's not as bad to be late with a YouTube video, you're wrong. Tons of YouTubers share that opinion, though, that it doesn't matter much if they're late, and that's a big reason why it's so easy to beat them.

If you're wondering, though, it's definitely better to be late than to post a bad video. There is never an excuse for posting a bad video. Both of those options are absolutely horrendous, though, and you should never do either.

Skip the Intro

No matter how long it is, even if it's only two seconds, you should never use a repeated intro sequence. This includes theme songs, opening credits, a quick channel logo that fills the screen — anything that seems like an intro, anything that's delaying the actual new content. A teaser can be fine, where we see a brief highlight from the video, but repeated intros are unacceptable.

The first seconds of a video are by far the most important and you can't waste them by annoying the audience with something they've already seen many times. Or, for new viewers, an intro signals to them that your channel probably sucks, since very few good channels use them anymore. In any case, you're delaying the content they clicked for, and there's no time to waste, not even a second. No one has any attention span anymore.

You should also try to avoid any dialogue that seems too introductory, especially if it's in any way delaying the content. If there's something important to tell the audience, don't do it in a talking head at the start of the video. First get into the actual content, as soon as humanly possible, and then work that dialogue into the early parts of the video.

This is a huge weakness of your competition, where they often spend the first minute or two talking about random nonsense or pointlessly describing what they're about to do before actually starting to do it. It's not only important for you to have nonstop dialogue, but it's also important to try to have something interesting going on visually for every second of the video, especially right at the start.

There's a reason why Netflix has a Skip Intro button and why they sometimes automatically skip the intro for you when they detect that you're binge-watching. Even for very popular theme songs, most people don't want to hear them over and over again.

And there's something else Netflix does even more brazenly that you also need to do:

Skip the Outro

I'm a decently smart person, but I can rarely figure out how to see the end credits of something on Netflix, because they're so good at instantly auto-playing the next thing. They intentionally make it confusing to do anything else, which annoys people like me who usually want to watch the credits. They do this because it dramatically raises the chances of keeping you watching for longer.

Why am I praising something that's confusing and annoying? Because you can achieve the same result without being confusing or annoying. You don't need end credits. When the content of your video is over, wrap it up as quickly as possible so the viewers can start watching the next one.

Never do anything that makes it seem like the video is over until it's actually over. The absolute sharpest declines in the retention graphs happen whenever the main purpose of the video ends. You must resist the urge to do a post-game show and talk about what just happened. Let it speak for itself. When the event ends, the video must end ASAP, because you're losing tons of viewers every second who won't make it to the end so they can watch the next one. You need them to watch the next one. And the one after that.

This is also why it's best to have a singular focus for each video. There are exceptions to this, but generally you should try to focus on one main event. For example, I once put two softball games in one episode, and even though that video has over a million views, practically no one has ever seen the second game that it featured. They all left when the first game ended.

It's incredible how many people end all of their videos with absolutely nothing, like a static image that promotes their social media accounts, usually with background music. They're also using end screens to link to their other videos, but that's pointless in their case because everyone already stopped watching. It's important to remember that the nonstop dialogue rule is for every single second of the video, and it's especially necessary for the beginning and end.

Please note, however, that I'm only referring to repeated, boring outros where you're showing the exact same footage. If you're doing something different each time, especially if it's interactive with the viewers in some way, like answering a question or letting them do the outro for you with footage they submitted, that can potentially be a great way to end your videos.

On a related note: Never do anything that makes it seem like your whole channel is over until it's actually over. Using titles like "Goodbye" or "I'm Quitting YouTube" might get you a lot of clicks in the short run, but they'll destroy your views in the future and you won't even realize what caused it because the drop will appear to be gradual after an initial spike. Many people will be curious about why you're quitting (or pretending to quit) and they'll briefly watch you more often because of that, but then they'll just think of you as a lying quitter. Believe it or not, this is a very common form of clickbait that silently kills channels. Don't even do this as a joke on April Fool's Day, because a significant percentage of your subscribers will see the title, forgetting what day it is, not click on the video, and then never click on any of your videos again because the title made them think you're a liar or quitter or both. People rarely investigate things. They make instant decisions based on limited info. Your whole goal is to never give the viewers a reason to dump you, and posting a video called "Goodbye" is like dumping them.

Ready Up

A minute ago I said that it's not only important for you to have nonstop dialogue, but it's also important to try to have something interesting going on visually for every second of the video, and that part needs to be highlighted with a star next to it. Let me give you a couple examples of what I'm talking about, from my real life videos and my gaming videos . . .

In my most popular series, I simply play softball with friends. We play a game and I do the commentary. Some facts about the softball series:

1. We have some good players, but no one elite, and some of us, like myself, are just plain bad.

2. It's usually a one camera shoot, hand held by me.

3. Humor is often injected, but the vast majority of each video is simply describing the action of the game, heavily focusing on the 20 or so errors that are usually made in each game.

4. There's no background music. It's just my voice.

5. I used to sometimes flash the score on the screen in text, but I haven't even done that in years. These videos are extremely low tech.

I could list a lot more things, but the point is that it doesn't seem like these videos should be popular. In fact, it seems like the type of series someone would make if they were trying to guarantee that no one would ever watch it. A common comment on the softball videos is "Why the hell was this in my recommendations?" But it wasn't in anyone's recommendations early on. The views were low for the first five months, until I made three key changes that boosted the watch time and made them go from getting about 20,000 views in their first month to over a million.

The first change was nonstop dialogue, the second was to sound much more excited about the game, and the third was to cut out almost everything that wasn't game action. But these cuts can't happen in the editing, since I do all of the commentary live, so I have to time everything perfectly on the field. For example, right when the pitcher releases the pitch I start my dialogue, and then I end my commentary for that play as soon as possible after the play ends, which often happens simultaneously. So I'd say, "The pitch to Benny — fly ball to left field and it's gonna be caught by Gabe for the second out," and I'd say "out" right when Gabe catches it, anticipating that in advance as he camps under the ball. The cut to the next play would happen instantly after the ball is caught, so that clip was entirely game action, and I do that for practically every play of the game, unless something special happens that warrants more focus.

This might seem simple and obvious, but the best advice usually is, especially if no one else is doing it. It took me about 50 games to figure that one out.

What this all comes down to is attempting to entertain the audience. These softball games may not be the most exciting thing in the world, but at least I'm not boring you with anything other than the action of the game. If you act interested in something, talk excitedly about it nonstop, and if you only show us the most interesting parts where there's something for us to visually follow, you're going to find an audience. All you really need to do is try.

Most of my gaming videos have no edits at all (more on that in the next chapter), which often makes it impossible to exclusively show game action, but I keep the percentage as high as possible by always "readying up." In most video games, there will often be various little moments or waiting screens that you have to skip past to get to the action, and it's called readying up when you hit whatever button is necessary to do so. In some baseball video games, for every at-bat they'll show a close up of the hitter as he steps into the batter's box, and this is almost always pointless and boring, something that you need to hit a button to skip past before the next pitch can be thrown. In the games I play, there's sometimes 100 moments like that per video where I need to quickly ready up to get to the action. There are of course exceptions where you'd want to show some of those scenes, but generally it's important to skip past them as quickly as possible.

Cheat Sheet

In my first year of recording gaming videos, I always wrote notes on a sheet that I'd tape below the camera to help remind me of the most important things that I had to do in those episodes. Unless you have an insanely good memory, you should definitely do the same. These should be bold headlines or even initials — just enough to remind you of what it is at a glance.

There's no excuse for continually forgetting meaningful things in your videos. Do whatever you reasonably can to avoid that. And a cheat sheet isn't just for gaming videos — you can refer to notes for any type of video you're making.

There's a million things you might write down, like "ready up" or "enthusiasm" or "schedule" or "promote IG," but I want to highlight one important duty that new YouTubers often forget, which is to talk about potential titles and thumbnails immediately after recording each video, or even during the filming, when possible. You have to do that when the content of the video is freshest in your mind, which can save tons of time later.

And again, I can sense that a lot of you are thinking this is the most obvious advice ever, like "Seriously? Take notes? I never would have thought of that, genius." But you'd be amazed at how many people have never tried this, including lots of successful YouTubers who constantly forget things and who would be even more successful if they used a cheat sheet.

Every video you make is a test and you need to study for it, and cheat if you have to.

Always Be Enthusiastic

In the *Lord of the Rings* books, there's something called the One Ring that dominates the story. Everyone wants to either use it or destroy it. Except this one dude named Faramir who says he wouldn't pick it up if he found it on the side of the road. In the films, they changed Faramir so that he initially does want the One Ring, because otherwise his attitude would make the audience feel like the Ring was far less important, like the whole story was meaningless. I love Faramir in the books, but if you want to be successful on YouTube, you need to be Film Faramir, not Book Faramir. You should never seem indifferent about anything that you're doing. You must always act like the focus of each video is incredibly important to you, like it has the power to destroy Middle-earth.

It's very hard to successfully fake enthusiasm, so you should be doing things that you actually enjoy. I love baseball and I love video games, so it's easy for me to act interested in playing a baseball video game, because I actually am. But that doesn't mean I'm not overdoing it at times to seem even more passionate than I might be feeling that day. It's fairly simple for anyone to jack up their enthusiasm from a 7 to a 9, but it requires incredible acting to go from a 3 to a 7. You should never even try that unless you've at least been nominated for a Daytime Emmy.

For YouTube, what you say is actually less important than how you say it. One of my favorite songs is "Hook" by Blues Traveler, which opens with this line: "It doesn't matter what I say, so long as I sing with inflection." To some degree, it's the same with YouTube. Your passion needs to come through, even if it's about something that doesn't seem very exciting. The audience will be interested because you're interested. It's far better to be passionate about something that bores others than to be bored by something that interests others.

So don't play a popular video game that you hate just because you think it will get views. Unless your emotional hatred for the game is the focus of the video — that could work great. Passion doesn't always have to be happy. We want to see emotions, and the more we see, the better.

Out of all my advice, this is the one that you're most likely to believe you're doing properly when you're really not. It's common for people to think their enthusiasm level is at an 8 when it's actually a 4 or

5. Here's how you can tell: The more often your facial expressions change, and the more dramatic those expressions are, the more enthusiastic you are. If we can't clearly see the emotions on your face, then you seem too bored.

This is also the one that you're most likely to refuse to do, because you think it's fake and because you hate fake YouTubers who always pretend to be freaking out about everything. I'm not saying to be like them. I'm saying to make sure it's a subject that you're genuinely interested in and then let your true emotions show — don't hide them. And yeah, maybe turn it up a notch or two if you're struggling to find the excitement. That doesn't make you a fake person. It makes you a professional entertainer.

If you ever significantly lose your passion for the type of videos you're making, you should stop making them, because your audience will notice. That's when you have to find something new that excites you. But if you do all of this correctly, even if you start to lose interest in the subject matter, your channel's success will keep you passionate about any videos you're making. For example, have you ever hated your job? Would you still hate it if it paid you $1,000 an hour? And when that doesn't work anymore, it shouldn't matter, because at that point you should already be set for life.

Congratulations on earning nine more badges!

CH. 3
BADGE

2%

You are now beating 78% of your competition.

CHAPTER FOUR

BLOWING UP

On June 27, 2019, I uploaded a video that got 458,495 views on that day alone, a one-day record for my channel. That one video made $2,485 that day, also a record at the time. But the interesting thing is that my channel made a total of $7,520 that day, which means that even on a day where I had my most viewed video ever, 67% of my revenue still came from all my other videos combined. If I didn't even post that record breaking video, my channel still would have made over $5,000 that day.

That's the point you need to get to, where new videos are just the cherry on top of the archive sundae.

The only way to do that is to first make a large archive of videos. On that record setting day, I had 326 different videos make at least $1. This is similar to a business model known as the long tail, where you sell small amounts of tons of different products, like Amazon does. Being a writer, though, I more often compare this to a prolific author who continues to sell lots of old books. For example, Stephen King made $25 million from book sales in 2010. Do you know how many new books he put out that year? Zero.

There are many things to take away from this, and here's the most important one:

You Haven't Failed Yet

A few months from now, after you've posted your first four videos, all of which have under 50 views, you'll be thinking two things:

1. I need to quit.

2. I should have never read this stupid book.

That's when you should re-read this section, because it barely matters how many views you get early on.

Go look at the first video posted by any super popular YouTube channel. It probably has over a million views. But do you know how many views it had in its first day? Probably under 100 and usually under 10. In most cases, that first video didn't start to gain traction until their YouTube channel started blowing up months or years later.

The only view count that really matters is how many views a video gets in its lifetime, not in its first day or week or year or even decade. Whenever anyone asks me how many views a particular video got, I think, "When YouTube goes out of business and shuts down, I'll let you know."

In over 99% of cases, after your first six months of trying hard at YouTube, you'll still have essentially no clue if you'll be successful or not. That's because six months is usually too soon to possibly blow up. So you're initially going to be doing a lot of work for very little pay while being almost completely in the dark about if it will all be worth it. This requires a lot of faith, and most people can't handle it and they quit way too early.

The truth is that you actually don't want to hit it big in the first six months, and here's why:

1. No matter how much time you spend preparing and making test videos, in almost all cases the videos you make in your seventh month will be far superior to the ones you make in your first. And, when you finally start to show up in people's recommendations, a high percentage of your first time viewers will be watching one of your latest videos, usually the start of a new series. This will give them a better first impression and a higher chance of putting you in their rotation than if you blew up in your first couple months and they were watching your early, inexperienced work.

2. More importantly, if you find success in your seventh month, you have seven months of videos for the new viewers to check out, which accumulates more views and again makes the viewers much more likely to put you in their rotation, because they've seen more of you.

3. It's better to hit it big after you're monetized so you can fully profit from it. Sometimes it takes weeks to get monetized after meeting the requirements, which could potentially cost you thousands of dollars if your initial algorithm love sends you millions of views, which happens all the time. If you follow this

book's advice, you should be monetized in the first six months.

Small YouTubers often complain about the algorithm hating them and never recommending their videos. It's laughable because in almost all of these cases their videos are so bad that they could spend $5 million on a Super Bowl ad for their channel and they'd literally only gain four subscribers from it. If the algorithm hates you, it's almost always because you're not ready yet, and you don't want it to like you until you are. Once it does like you, your early videos can go from having 47 views to a million. You're not wasting your time on them, or at least you can't know that yet.

This is a big additional reason why you need to like the subject of your videos, why you need to enjoy producing them, because you'll most likely need to make at least 100 of them before you can form a solid opinion about if you're succeeding or not.

On a related note, if you're starting a new channel, I highly recommend not posting about it on social media until after it blows up or until after you've consistently posted videos for six months. It's actually a big sign of potential failure for a channel when they spread the news about it on social media after only uploading their first video. All that does is annoy people who assume you'll never stay consistent with it, because that's what happens in over 99% of cases when someone tells people about their new YouTube channel — it's dead in a month. You'll get way more of your followers to actually check out your channel if you can say that you've posted 100+ videos already and that it's starting to take off.

You Need a Schedule

Viewers love schedules. They want to know exactly when your videos go up and they want to be there the second they do. This isn't because they want to make the first comment. It's because people love being a fan of something and being part of a community. Just imagine if the New England Patriots had no schedule and they just randomly played their games at weird times. It's not quite as dumb as that to not have a schedule for your videos, but almost.

Like I said in the previous chapter, though, if you have a schedule, you have to stick to it. If you're never late, a schedule is a huge benefit to your channel. If only 99% of your videos go up on time, it's still a net positive. If 98% of your videos are on time, your schedule is now slightly hurting you. If 90% of your videos are on time, your schedule is killing your channel because of your lateness pissing off way too many of your subscribers. If 70% of your videos are on time, your channel is probably hopeless because you clearly don't give a crap about it.

When was the last time you heard of a TV show being late for a scheduled episode? Never, right? There's a reason for that. They know what kind of damage that would do, so they usually complete each episode weeks or months before it airs. You don't have to be that far ahead, but you should try to always be at least a few days ahead of schedule. This is of course impossible for some channels that deal with current events, like daily vlogs. Even then, try to finish every video as early as possible in case any problems occur.

It's only helpful to have a schedule if you promote the hell out of it. Talk about it early in every video and plaster it everywhere you can, like in your channel banner and in a pinned comment for each video. If the audience doesn't know about your schedule, then it's not doing you any good.

How often should you post videos? It depends on what kind of videos you make and how long they take and what the status of your channel is at the time. In general, though, you should post videos as often as possible.

If it takes you an average of five hours to make a video, and if you can only spare 15 hours per week, then you should upload three videos a week. If it takes you 15 hours to make a video, which is all of your available weekly time, then you need to figure out different kinds of videos that can be made much faster. Unless your videos are insanely good and become a viral phenomenon, once a week is not enough. And neither is three times a week, really, but that can be acceptable early on just to gather enough information to see if you want to pursue it full time.

Ideally, in a perfect world, you should post three videos every day. That's what I did for most of 2016, and it's a big reason why YouTube recommended my videos. I even tried four videos a day for a few weeks, but I feel like that was overkill and not worth the effort, because it crossed the line of bombarding my audience with too many uploads that they couldn't keep up with.

There are times, however, when you should consider posting four or more videos in a day, like the week when a very popular new video game comes out that your audience loves, or the week before Christmas when ad revenue is sky high (more on that in the next chapter). Also, if you're desperate to finally hit it big and get recommended, you should consider posting five or six videos every day for a while at some point, because the algorithm seems to love channels that post a lot. But I only suggest trying that overkill strategy if you're already getting at least 1,000 views per video in their first week and if you already have at least 100 total videos. Yes, the algorithm loves channels that upload a lot, but it's still almost never going to recommend a channel that hasn't shown significant signs of life yet. You need to first build a decent sized audience on your own before the algorithm will do the rest for you.

In fact, unless you have all the time in the world and you really love making videos, I wouldn't recommend going beyond daily and posting more than one video per day until all of your recent videos are getting at least 100 views in their first week. The algorithm isn't going to care that you're posting two videos per day if only a few people are watching them.

When you start showing up in recommended videos, it's the equivalent of YouTube giving you lots of free advertising, and the algorithm is designed to use that ad space as wisely as possible. The numbers need to show that you're a good bet, and it's very difficult to achieve those numbers quickly, since one of the key factors is Total Watch Time, which requires lots of videos and a decent amount of views. Luckily, that's not the only factor. Watch Time Percentage is also huge, along with how often you post and a myriad of other stats. It's certainly possible to get recommended after only 20 videos, or even after only one video, but the odds keep shooting up as you post more.

Many of you are thinking that it's an absurd impossibility for you to post three videos a day, and if you make certain types of videos, you might be right. But I once thought the same thing about my channel.

From early November of 2015 to mid-January of 2016, I only uploaded two videos per week, which were all just softball games that I played with friends. At the time, they were getting about 20,000 views each and only making around $15 each (my ad revenue was terrible back then, for reasons I'll explain in the next chapter). But then, on January 20, 2016, I started posting gaming videos, and that changed everything. They were far easier to make than the softball series and they were getting similar views early on.

As I learned how to edit quicker, for both the gaming videos and softball, I started posting more and more. Shortly after going to a twice daily schedule in March of 2016, the algorithm started liking me and my views went through the roof. I then did something very important that you must remember to do yourself when the time comes:

Ride the Wave

When my channel started blowing up, I bumped my production up from two videos per day to three and I did everything I could to keep the momentum going, because it's incredibly easy for it to die out. When you start hitting it big, that's when it's by far the most important time to not screw up — to not be late, to not try anything weird with your videos, to avoid anything that could possibly upset your new audience. You should also start producing more videos instantly, especially if you're not yet daily at the time.

If you're only making three videos per week and you start getting tons of views out of nowhere, do anything you can to immediately go daily. Consider quitting your job, if need be, because you might not get this chance again. If you're out of sight, you're out of mind, and your new subscribers will have lost interest in you by the time your next video goes up if you aren't posting at least once a day. In my opinion, being daily is literally 20 times better than uploading three videos per week, despite it only being about twice as many videos.

You'd be amazed at how many people completely fail to ride the wave. They suddenly go from getting 100 views per video to 10,000, and what do they do in response? They stop uploading, or they start posting different types of videos from the ones that were getting big views, and within weeks they're down to 300 views per video, which feels like less than zero compared to the 10,000 they were getting. There are many possible reasons for why they do this, like being scared of having so many people watching them, or being afraid of success in general because it will completely change their life, but I think the most common reason for failing to ride the wave is that they don't realize it's a wave. They think the views will always be high now, like they've just signed a five-year contract in a corner office. There's no contract with YouTube, but you do have a boss — the audience — and they'll fire you instantly if you take them for granted. Don't spike the ball on the 1-yard line.

Before you start to blow up, you should think of those early videos as pre-season games and yourself as a rookie who's struggling to make the team. So those videos are still very important — they're not just practice — but when you actually make the team and you're starting on Opening Day, that's when it really counts and you have to work harder than ever to keep your dream job.

A big part of riding the wave is learning how to make videos faster so you can maintain a busy schedule. My early softball videos took about eight hours to edit and they weren't even good. Nowadays softball takes about one hour to edit. My early Road to the Show videos took about two hours to edit. Now they take about one minute, literally. I'll explain that in a second, but first I want to say that editing will get easier and quicker over time. There are a million different tips I could give for that, but it all comes down to personal experience.

Early on I didn't know what people would like and what I should include in the videos, so I debated about things for ages. I was so worried about making good videos that I took forever to get everything just right. I also wasn't an expert with the editing software, which slowed things down, and my computer sucked, which really slowed things down. Over time, you'll learn what your audience likes, you'll build confidence, you'll master the software, and eventually you'll get a better computer.

No-Edit Videos

Most of the gaming videos on my channel were made with essentially no editing. I film those videos in a live-streaming style where I play a video game for 10-15 minutes, talking nonstop, and then all I have to do is chop off the stuff before and after. For those types of videos, the most difficult part of the editing is simply syncing up the dialogue and the gameplay, but even that only takes one minute. I haven't even watched most of my videos, and I'm the only one who's ever edited them.

If you really want to supercharge your video production, figure out a way to do a series like that, where you're doing something of interest while talking for 10-20 minutes straight. Video games are usually the best way to do this, but there are many possibilities. Some games, and modes within games, lend themselves more to this style. You have to find the ones that work best for your channel.

These types of videos will rarely be the breakout hits that make you blow up initially, but they're the key to a large passive income after you've earned an audience from videos that are harder or more expensive to make. Let's say you gain some traction with vlogs or pranks or anything that takes a long time to produce, and you suddenly have thousands of people who want to watch your videos, but it's literally impossible to make two of them per day, and for some channels even making two videos per week would be a challenge. That's when you need to figure out videos that are much simpler to make. I personally have found ways to make videos with essentially no editing at all, and it's not necessary for you to do that, but you should be able to discover videos that take far less time to produce than your main series.

Once you have an audience that likes you and wants to see more of you, a certain percentage of them will watch you do practically anything, as long as you're clearly trying to entertain them and as long as you stay in the same genre.

For example, if you built an audience from highly edited woodworking tutorials that in some cases took weeks to make, you should try a daily series where you show unedited footage as you document the entire process of building various items while talking to the viewers nonstop. Film for 90 minutes while you're constructing a barstool, and break that into seven videos of 10-15 minutes each, with a short break between each episode to tell yourself ideas for possible titles and thumbnails for the one you just finished. Or pick out the coolest parts of making certain projects and post unedited videos of doing just that portion of the job.

An even better idea, though, would be to play a woodworking video game while talking nonstop. And yes, I just googled it and there is a woodworking video game, and multiple YouTube videos of playing that game have gotten over a million views. I told you there's an audience for almost everything.

For the no-edit videos, you can choose to exclusively talk about the subject at hand or you could just say whatever's on your mind, although I suggest staying away from controversial topics. Try to inject humor whenever possible and make sure that the audience feels like they know you.

Remember, the goal is to post more videos so you can get more views. It's a common misconception that the most important YouTube stat is how many subscribers you have. In general, with some exceptions, total views are infinitely more important than subscribers. A large number of subscribers and fame can help you get better sponsorship deals, but even then sponsors care much more about how many views they can expect from the sponsored video than they do about how many subscribers you have. And in terms of YouTube ad revenue, subscribers are meaningless. All that matters for revenue is how many commercials are seen during your videos (more on this in the next chapter).

It's always frustrating to see popular YouTubers who have never posted a lot of videos. There are thousands of channels that have over 100,000 subscribers but less than 100 total uploads. Many of those YouTubers have secondary channels where they upload more often, but for those who don't, they're leaving a huge amount of money on the table.

Let's look at two channels:

Channel A has 2.1 million subscribers and they post one video per week that averages 500,000 views, so they get 26 million total views per year from new videos.

Channel B has 84,000 subscribers and they upload three videos per day that average 24,000 views, which totals 26.3 million views per year from new videos.

Channel B is getting more total views and probably making more ad revenue, even though Channel A has 25 times more subscribers and 21 times more views per video.

If you're Channel A and you're averaging 500,000 views per video, any decent effort no-edit videos that you make would probably average over 70,000 views, so if you put out three of them per day, your annual views would jump from 26 million to over 100 million and you're suddenly making four times more money. And that's only looking at the views from new videos each year. The difference would be even more stark when considering subsequent years and all the added views from the greatly expanded archive of videos.

You might be wondering if you should make a second channel for your no-edit videos or if you should just post them on your main channel. I think it depends on how good the simple to make videos are and how different they are from your main series. If they're nowhere near as good, and/or if they're not exactly in the same genre, you should put them on a second channel and just promote them heavily on your main channel. For me, my most popular individual videos are where I play softball with friends, but I get more total views from my videos of playing a baseball video game, most of which have no editing in recent years. I post all of those videos on my main channel.

When making my no-edit gaming videos, I almost always film many of them in one recording session, which makes the whole process go much faster. For example, from start to finish — and when I say start,

I mean the second I start recording the gameplay, and when I say finish, I mean with absolutely everything, including uploading the videos to YouTube and completing the titles and thumbnails — I can make seven videos in five hours.

But it's actually a lot faster than that, because half of that time is simply waiting for the computer to do things. So it's only two and a half hours of work, because I can do anything while waiting for renders and uploads, like watch Netflix. If you can be fully engaged in an episode of *Stranger Things* while doing it, then it doesn't count as work. But even for those two and a half hours of "work," two of those hours are literally spent playing my favorite video game. So it's really only 30 minutes of actual work that I don't enjoy doing — 10 minutes of editing and 20 minutes of making titles and thumbnails — to complete seven videos. Which, for me currently, should make a combined total of somewhere around $3,000 in their first year alone and $10,000 in their first decade. For 30 minutes of simple technical work and two hours of playing a video game.

Jobs don't get much better than this.

Congratulations on earning four more badges!

You are now beating 86% of your competition.

CHAPTER FIVE

MAKING MONEY

M ost successful YouTube channels make money in three key ways: ad revenue, sponsored videos, and merchandise. I'm planning to change this soon, but up to this point I've made over 99% of my money from YouTube ad revenue alone. Financially, that's not the smartest approach, but I think it's good to know that it's very possible to get rich on YouTube without doing sponsored videos or promoting merch.

Personally, I've never been comfortable with being a salesman. Along with doing YouTube for a living, I've also written comic books and screenplays since I was a teenager. My comic book company has had a booth at the San Diego Comic-Con for decades and I generally hate being at the booth, because it means I have to talk to humans and try to sell them stuff. In an attempt to get out of this to some degree, I started putting a one sentence description of the story on the back cover of all my graphic novels, which I would then simply point at whenever anyone asked me what those books were about.

So I'm not a salesman and I'm currently not an expert on how to diversify your income. I believe I am an expert, however, on how to maximize YouTube ad revenue without alienating your audience, and here's how:

Midrolls

If your channel is monetized, a commercial might play before and after your videos. If your video is over eight minutes long, you can also place midroll ads during each video where a commercial might play. For many years, videos needed to be 10 minutes long to have midrolls, and you should continue to act like the rule is still 10 minutes for these two reasons:

1. In all those years under the old rule, nearly every successful channel almost exclusively posted videos that were at least 10 minutes long. The result is that YouTube viewers now generally see videos that are under 10 minutes as being amateur garbage, even if it's only on a subconscious level, and you'll get fewer clicks for those videos. It seems crazy, but if that little timestamp in the bottom right corner says 9:46, that screams TRASH, while 10:07 means it at least has a chance to be good.

2. Even if that first point didn't exist, you'd still want your videos to be over 10 minutes because a longer video means more watch time and more ad views.

So yes, you only need eight minutes for midrolls, and if every once in a while you make a video that's between 8 and 10 minutes, that's not the end of the world, but you should always shoot for a minimum of 10.

My videos are generally 15-20 minutes, but if I'm making a video that I suspect will get tons of views, I usually try to make it closer to 30 minutes to really maximize watch time and ad views.

Much more important than the video's length, though, is how many midrolls to use and where to place them, and here are my rules for that:

1. Never place a midroll in the first minute.

2. Never place midrolls within one minute of each other.

3. Never place a midroll after the 6:00 mark.

4. Never place a midroll unless it's directly after an entertaining moment or right when it seems to the audience like an entertaining moment is about to occur.

5. Never place the first midroll until something pretty entertaining has already happened, preferably something that would make the viewer laugh. It really upsets viewers to see a midroll pop up before they feel like they've been entertained in any real way. Which is another great reason to never do intros and to get right into the action as soon as possible.

So ideally, if something entertaining happens at the right times, here's where you'd want to post midrolls in a perfect dream world: 1:01, 2:02, 3:03, 4:04, 5:05. But it will never work out that way, and if a video doesn't have any clearly entertaining moments early on, then you shouldn't be using any midrolls, because they'll just kill your watch time.

You might be confused by this advice, because I've personally never seen any YouTuber do midrolls like this, other than myself and my friends. If you're wondering why it's best to put a bunch of midrolls in the first six minutes of a video and none late in a video, this is why:

1. No one's watching after the first six minutes. Midrolls can't make you any money if no one ever sees them. I'm of course exaggerating when I say "no one," but the point is that you need these ads to be seen, so you need to place them when a high percentage of your viewers are still watching.

2. You might ask what harm it does to place some commercials late in videos as well, to make a little extra money. The harm comes from viewers seeing a million little yellow lines at the bottom of the video that designate when an ad might play, which scares them off, hurts your watch time, and does so much damage that those late midrolls are actually losing you money instead of making you money.

3. Compare this to the way most YouTubers use midrolls. Let's look at a 21-minute video.

Most successful YouTubers would do one of three things: They'd place one midroll at about the 10:00 mark, they'd place two midrolls at about the 7:00 and 14:00 marks, or they'd place three midrolls at about the 6:00, 12:00 and 18:00 marks. In all three of those cases, there probably isn't a single ad placed during a time when more than half of their viewers are still watching. As compared to my strategy, where I usually have four midrolls placed when more than half of viewers are still watching. And yes, viewing more commercials annoys some people, but my channel doesn't seem to have significantly more complaints about midrolls than any other channel. I think that's because they're placed in good spots and because you're done with them after you get past the first six minutes.

4. Because it works. In June of 2021, my RPM (revenue per thousand views) was over $9 with an average watch time of 7:44 per video. On June 21st, 2021, my channel made $9,909.34 from less than 900,000 views. I'd give you more exact figures about my RPM, but I don't think YouTube's guidelines allow me to do that. In any case, for my genre of videos, this is a high RPM, and my average watch time wasn't much higher back when I had no midrolls.

5. Keep in mind that placing a midroll doesn't mean that a commercial will definitely play at that point. It just means a commercial might play. Sometimes you'll only have one ad play for every five or six yellow lines, so you want to make sure those lines are early in the video when people are still watching.

I very much wish that I knew all of this earlier in my YouTube career. For various reasons I didn't monetize my videos at all until five years in, and I never placed a single midroll until late August of 2016, when my channel already had 120 million views in the first eight months of that year. It wasn't until December of 2016 that I started heavily experimenting with adding more than one or two midrolls. I threw away roughly half a million dollars by not utilizing this strategy earlier.

I didn't use midrolls earlier because I thought it would anger the viewers. And of course it did, but nowhere near enough to matter, especially when I wasn't also annoying them with sponsored videos or merchandise promotion. People are used to seeing ads everywhere. That's how the world works. They might act upset in the comments, but the ones who are actually commenting are the ones you have to worry about the least. They're not going anywhere.

I'm not certain, by the way, that my midroll strategy is the best way to go. It's simply what's worked for me. And you might notice that lots of my videos don't precisely follow this strategy. That's either because they were made before I settled on this strategy and I haven't gone back and changed them, or it's because I'm still experimenting at times.

When to Upload

To maximize views and revenue, you need to post your videos at the best times. And I don't just mean time of day, but especially time of year.

For time of day, any time between 9 AM Eastern and 9 PM Eastern can work pretty well for a mostly American audience. You just want to avoid the late night hours. I currently think that 10 AM Eastern is the best time to post. When I upload three videos per day, I post them at 10 AM, 1 PM and 4 PM Eastern.

For time of year, this will heavily depend on your specific genre, but you obviously want to upload more videos when views are high and when RPM is high.

You can google this to try to find a more detailed calendar, but here's a basic rundown of what I've experienced for RPM: January and February are the worst months of the year (except for a few days starting with Super Bowl Sunday when RPM is huge), March is good (especially late March), April is average, May is pretty good, June is great (especially late June), July through September is below average, October is good, and November and December are great, especially the week of Thanksgiving and the week before Christmas.

In terms of views, you'll need to learn when your audience is most likely to watch your type of content. For a baseball channel like mine, that's mostly mid-March to mid-July. The other eight months are a struggle to attract viewers. But five of those other eight months have low RPM anyway, so for an established channel like mine that doesn't need to fight anymore to build up an audience, I mostly just don't post anything when views and RPM are both low.

I've heard of YouTubers who upload more often than usual during the worst months for views and RPM because they feel like they have to grind the hardest in those times to still make a good amount of money for each of those months. I think that's ridiculous. It doesn't matter how much money you make each month. It matters how much money you make each year. You don't want to waste a bunch of videos during a time when RPM is low and when not many people are watching content like yours. You need to save your energy to pump out lots of videos when views and RPM are high. If you have great ideas for videos that could go up at any time, save them for the high view and RPM months.

For example, June is usually my biggest month because views are at their highest for a baseball channel and RPM is great too, so I just put out 60 videos in June of 2021, as compared to the zero I posted in January. And, knowing that views and RPM would start dropping rapidly in early July, I mostly tried to put out my best videos in early to mid-June so that they'd have a few weeks of ideal conditions before their views would start to naturally drop off anyway. Remember, if you do all of this correctly, it's not just the first day that matters for these videos. They'll continue to accumulate views for forever. But they'll still almost always get a large percentage of their views in the first few weeks that they're up.

To be clear, I'm definitely not saying that you shouldn't post videos in January. I'm saying that you need to be aware of the good and bad times to post and respond accordingly. If you're still trying to initially blow up, you should treat every day like it's a great time to post. And if you absolutely adore making videos, feel free to continue uploading three videos per day for the next 50 years. But if you're like me and need a break every once in a while, be sure to take it at the right time.

Throughout most of each year, if you checked my channel's recent public stats, you'd think it was dying. I get comments like that all the time. "It's so sad that this channel died." That's because they're looking at a slow time of year when I'm on a break. The reality is that my channel just had its best April ever, best May ever, and best June ever. You need to ignore ignorant comments and stay focused on doing what's best for your channel.

Family Friendly

It's very difficult to get big on YouTube without being family friendly. If your content would scare off advertisers, YouTube is not going to recommend your videos. It's that simple. If you perfectly do everything that this book suggests, but your videos are about a fight club that you started in your basement, you're not going to get a million subscribers.

Not only should your content be family friendly, but so should your comments. And I'm not just talking about the comments you personally make — I'm talking about the entire comment section for your videos. People spend a lot of time reading comments. Some people exclusively watch YouTube videos while simultaneously reading the comments, and those comments will heavily sway their opinion about the video and help them to decide about adding you to their rotation. This is your comment section. You control it. You can delete horrible comments and you should.

Titles & Thumbnails

The most important thing I can tell you about titles and thumbnails is to repeat what I said earlier about how you don't want a lot of views for a bad video. You also don't really want a lot of views for an average video. You only even want to try to get a lot of views for good videos.

The better a video is, the more you're allowed to clickbait. If it's a great video, no one will ever be mad about clickbait. Get the most views you possibly can for great videos, without going completely insane. You should never flat out lie in a title or thumbnail, but it's OK to incorrectly imply things if the video is good enough.

My thumbnails are extremely simple. They're almost always just a frame from the video itself, and then I add an episode number in the corner somewhere. My channel would probably benefit from fancier thumbnails, but I'm bad at making such things and I've been hesitant to hire anyone to help. I think the simple thumbnails work decently with the old school feel of my videos, but they can't be ideal for getting clicks.

Never put anything of importance, especially any text, near the bottom right corner of the thumbnail, because the timestamp might block it.

Titles generally do best when they highlight one key moment. Titles are not newspaper headlines. They shouldn't try to summarize the video. You need to draw people in with one cool or funny thing in the title and thumbnail, and then it's a battle to make them watch the whole video when all they wanted to see was one moment.

For good videos that you think might get a lot of views, you should usually make multiple different thumbnails (with multiple titles to go with them), just in case the first one doesn't perform well. I once tried 15 different combinations of titles and thumbnails until I finally found one that took off for a video that I wanted to get a ton of views.

You should consider the amount of time that you spend on titles and thumbnails to be like your marketing budget for that video. If you think the video is great enough to provide a huge return on your investment, then spend hours on that title/thumbnail, spend days on it even. On the other hand, if the video is mediocre, barely good enough to post, don't spend more than one minute on it.

I see lots of YouTubers doing the exact opposite of this. They'll quickly make the title/thumb for the great video because lots of awesome things happened in that video and it was simple to pick one and run with it. In the mediocre video, nothing of interest happened, so the YouTuber agonizes over how to promote it and often goes with something very clickbaity, which is the last thing you want for a video like that.

One issue here is that the YouTuber is often content with a certain high number of views that they can count on getting for the great video, when they should be trying harder to get even more views for it. Yes, your first idea for the title/thumbnail for this great video is decent and you'll get a million views, but there might be a better option that will get you four million instead. That's way more worthy of your time than trying to figure out how to bump the mediocre video up from 200,000 to 400,000, especially when you shouldn't even want more views for that video at all. That video's probably hurting your channel, but you feel obligated to post it. Which happens, I get it. But that doesn't mean you should feel obligated to make sure it gets a lot of views. Never be embarrassed by a low view count. Be embarrassed by the crappy content of the video.

Congratulations on earning four more badges!

You are now beating 94% of your competition.

CHAPTER SIX

DEALING WITH SUCCESS

P eople say that you shouldn't let success change you. That's stupid. You need to let success make you a happier person.

The problem with success is that it makes you want more of it, to the point where some people are never satisfied. Like anything else that feels good, you have to be careful to not get addicted.

I know people with a million subscribers who were far happier about their channel back when it had 700 subscribers. They're usually unhappy not because their channel is in some horrible decline, but because another channel in their genre is doing better.

I'm a very competitive person. I think competition is generally a great thing. It makes life more exciting and it can motivate you to incredible heights. Literally the subtitle for this book tells you to "beat all your competition." But you need to make sure that you keep some kind of logical perspective about where you are and where you came from.

Never let success be more stressful than failure. Never allow yourself to be one of those insufferable people who achieve all their dreams and aren't even happy about it.

Mental Preparation

It's very important to realize that things won't always go well. It pains me to say that because it's so simple and obvious, but when your channel is first blowing up, it's really easy to fool yourself into thinking that it will always keep growing.

In 2016, there was a stretch where my channel's total views increased for 18 consecutive weeks. I somehow thought there was a good chance that that streak would never end, that the channel would keep growing until I died of extreme old age. When the drop off finally happened, it blindsided me. I started questioning everything I was doing and I scrambled to figure out how to fix it. But there was nothing to fix. I had simply reached a bad time of year for baseball content, which I wasn't aware of yet.

It's extremely important to make adjustments, when necessary, in every aspect of life. But be careful not to overreact. When a popular series suddenly has a decline in views, even a steep decline, that doesn't always mean that you need to change something. It definitely doesn't mean that you should quit that series and upload something totally different instead. All that will do is turn a steep decline into a nosedive that your channel might never recover from.

Gratitude

Let's say you're a broke loser. Everything in your life sucks. You love basketball, though, so one day you start up a YouTube channel all about basketball. You play NBA 2K, you play pickup games with your friends, and suddenly you've got 100,000 subscribers and you can move out of your grandma's attic. At this point, YouTube and the NBA ask you to take part in a series of live chats for NBA games that are exclusively aired on YouTube. All you have to do is talk in the chat with other basketball YouTubers about games that you probably would have been watching anyway. And here's where it gets interesting: You turn this offer down because they weren't offering any money and you feel like they weren't respecting the value that you bring.

Please don't be that person.

Be grateful to people and organizations who helped you get to where you are. And this isn't just about being a good person — it's best for business too. Aren't you going to want YouTube and the NBA to like you in that scenario? That could lead to much bigger things. If that's me, I'm treating YouTube and the NBA as if they both saved my life in Vietnam.

Be grateful to the viewers too. And this is a very minor thing, but I suggest referring to them as viewers, as opposed to fans. We're YouTubers. We're not Justin Bieber. Although he started out as a YouTuber just like us, so maybe you'll get there one day. But until you're selling out arenas, you just have viewers.

Strong Handshake

You need one.

Congratulations on earning three more badges!

You are now beating 99% of your competition.

The final 1% comes from your skills as an entertainer. At the start of this book, I said you needed to be at least a 5 on the 1-10 entertainer scale. If you're a 5 and you do everything this book suggests, you're now beating 99.5% of your competition, and that's as high as you can go. If you're a 10, you're beating 100% of your competition.

If you're a 4, however, that doesn't mean you're beating 99.4% of your competition. You need more talent than that to make any of this work. If you're a 4, you're probably only beating 85% of your competition. Which is probably not enough to make a living.

It's of course impossible to know exactly where you are on that scale, but you should have a pretty good idea. I think I'm a 7. You might check out my videos and think I'm a 3. You might think, "This is the guy I'm supposed to learn from? His videos are trash." And that's awesome. That means you should be able to do way better.

I wrote this book because people constantly ask me how I've done so well on YouTube. A big reason why they ask is because my videos aren't the type that would normally do well. I think that shows how well my system works. It wouldn't be nearly as impressive if I had the gaming skills of Ninja or if I was a daily vlogger who was always flexing on people with videos about $28,000 airplane seats.

If I can do it, you can do it. There's nothing holding you back. You just have to try.

ABOUT THE AUTHOR

Bobby Crosby is a writer and YouTuber. His YouTube channel has more than 1.3 million subscribers and over 700 million views. He is the author of the graphic novels *Marry Me* (recently adapted into a feature film starring Jennifer Lopez), *Last Blood*, and *Dreamless*, as well as the comic strips *+EV* and *Pupkin*. Bobby lives in Los Angeles with his girlfriend.